The World of Art Education According To Lanier

Vincent Lanier

1991

National Art Education Association
1916 Association Drive
Reston, Virginia 22091-1590

Good evidence of how that dialogue would proceed is contained in Lanier's own approach to art education theory. It is invariably construed as a debate with his colleagues; it is always focussed on fundamental issues arising from the life of art; and it is disputatious and critical. Indeed, it could be seen as the closest we get in art education theory to a Socratic dialogue; so much so that, at times, Lanier himself must feel relieved that the practice of making unpopular philosophers drink hemlock has gone out of fashion.*

---

* Ted Bracey, "Art Education for the 2020's: One That is Truly Moral," *Canadian Revue of Art Education*, Vol. 17, No. 1, 1990, p. 45, 46.

Contents

The World of Art Education According to Lanier   5

Philosophical Bases and Derivative Principles   9
    Democratizing the Range of Aesthetic Objects   14
    Eliminating Developmental Purposes   15
    Aesthetics as the Curriculum   16
    Contextualism in Aesthetic Response   23

One View of Our History   25

Randomly Organized Opinions   37
    The Apotheosis of Art Education   37
    Politics and Art Education   39
    Art Teacher Education   43
    Multicultural Art Education   45
    Outsiders in Art Education   47
    Newer Media   49
    Repeat Performance   53
    Coda   55

The World of Art Education According to Lanier

One of the several significant disappointments of advanced age is the absence of that illuminating wisdom the years are alleged to bequeath. At least, that is so for me. As I enter my seventh decade, I am somewhat ruefully aware that I cannot answer with authority any of the vital questions either of life in general or of art education in particular, with which I have dealt professionally for 40 years. True, I have stored a respectable amount of knowledge and do, more often than not, exhibit that all too common hardening of the arteries of opinion. However, neither I nor, likely, anyone else, will confuse either of these two accomplishments with wisdom.

Nevertheless, I am not at all reluctant to take this opportunity that the National Art Education Association (NAEA) has generously provided in this monograph, to proffer some of that knowledge and many of those opinions. The only stipulations I must impose are the following: I may sometimes be inordinately candid in these pages, not sparing the feelings of my colleagues. I will claim that age and tenure excuse even an offensive honesty.

My second stipulation is that I keep this monograph quite short. NAEA most liberally offered a 150-200 page length to these papers, which is nearly enough for a major textbook in the field. However, although I am vain enough to believe that I have at least that much to say if not much more, and I am convinced that the truth as I see it must be promulgated as widely and as frequently as possible, I am also aware that a great deal of what I might say is already in print. Indeed, I have been most fortunate in being able to publish the major portion of what I have written, either in journals in the field or in book form.

There was a time in the sixties and seventies when what I submitted to *Studies* was initially rejected as unscholarly, scholarship being equated in the thinking of editors and reviewers with numbers of footnotes, the presence of statistical displays, and unswerving sobriety. I remember, for example, that "The Five Faces of Art Education" had a particularly rough time before it was finally accepted. On the other hand, I have received much excellent criticism from unknown colleagues in review form and appreciate their loyalty to scholarly principles. Collectively, they taught me to strive for leaner and meaner prose and to abjure the circumlocution. Some have characterized what I write as easy and flowing, but I must confess that whatever its caliber, it is just damn hard work; while I never begrudged the effort, I would not wish it diminished. As a consequence, I have a great respect for all writings, including poor ones. Even a bad book is a major accomplishment.

Third, I intend to digress when such material seems informative. Occasional reminiscences that highlight a point of our history may help to lend an air of authenticity and humanity to what might otherwise be turgidly didactic. I remember from my teaching that students enjoyed the reassurance that Lowenfeld admired the well turned ankle; it made these dusty textbook characters more three-dimensional and, thus, more human. Ideas are wonderful things, but they are thought of and held by people, who give them coloration or timbre. David Templeton called the forties The Age of Heroes with good reason; the larger than life characters who were the major figures of art education at the time not only colorized ideas, but almost literally sold them to the public like breakfast cereal. It seems as if ever since that time we have been muddling along in an era of pygmies.

The customary procedure in comprehensive statements like this one is to start at the beginning. If I am to do that, I shall have to describe as succinctly as possible some of my philosophical beliefs, having insisted in earlier writings that ideas about art and its teaching can often and should whenever possible be traceable to varieties of basic premise. People do not have to be consistent; one can firmly hold one set of ideas in metaphysics or ethics, and yet hold views in more limited areas such as art or art education that are not consonant with those original beliefs. This is, perhaps, particularly true of people in the arts, whose ideological heritage in our culture appears to contain a considerable amount of anti-intellectualism. Art people as students are often encouraged to grunt and emote, thinking being what our British colleagues might call bad form.

On the other hand, the educated person, in any discipline, courts consistency. Such a person usually believes that an examined life requires the maximum of dovetailing among the various ideas about the world which all of us develop. I subscribe to this opinion and try to comb my beliefs periodically (though not always successfully, I am sure), in the hope of expanding such consistency. I would urge all of us to do likewise, the most diligently with those ideas upon which we set the greatest store. This spring cleaning of the mind, along with omnivorous reading, are the signal hallmarks of the educated person.

Philosophical Bases and Derivative Principles

I am a materialist in my metaphysics and believe in the method of science when it is applicable and reason when it is not. I have occasionally run into people who are startled by my rather bald declaration of materialism and who suspect my seriousness. The conversation usually goes something like this:

"Do you really mean it?"

"Yes, I do."

"But then ... but then there is no ..."

"Yes, Virginia, and there is no Santa Claus either."

Those who raise such a question do not seem to realize that materialism is a perfectly respectable intellectual position, as long as it is not confused with the mundane, bastardized meaning of the term, which is associated in popular language with greed and sensuality. I would guess that this contamination of meaning is no accident, but, rather, a deliberate misrepresentation, for, in fact, a materialist can have moral views almost identical to those of, for example, a Christian, although their origin would be empirical instead of spiritual or theological.

Materialism means quite literally that all things in the universe, including ourselves and our ideas, are made up of matter in one form or another in the process of motion and change. In the words of one of the Barrymores in a play whose name escapes me: "That's all there is, there isn't any more." Thus, the materialist looks for explanations for both personal and social phenomena in the material world of objective reality of which ideas are a reflection. Further, the most efficient method yet devised for insuring accuracy in that reflection is the method of science. It is quite fashionable today to cast suspicions on the efficacy of science as a method of explaining objective reality. One can fault science because it cannot tell us what the universe is, how it came to be, and where it is going, which is true. Or one can assert that science falls down as a method in less intimidating tasks, like telling us about the nature of art, for example. This charge is also true. On the other hand and more to the point, what science does tell us is knowledge on which we stake our lives every single day: by travel in aircraft, by submission to surgery, or, indeed, by imbibing any kind of medication. If science is dependable enough to trust with our lives, I see no reason why we cannot accept that it is effective in less sensitive contexts.

Fortunately, most of us already know the procedures of scientific method since it has been useful to train workers who can turn the wheels of industry. Hence, science is taught in our schools, but only as a means of dealing with physical events. Beliefs such as moral principles are supposed to originate in other less earthly spheres and as a consequence are both absolute and immutable and are often totally disconnected from the social context to which they are related. Thus, for example, according to this view to be homeless is to possess some inherent shortcoming; it has nothing to do with corporate greed or governmental indifference.

My conception of moral value seems to derive, as well as I can trace it, from what is loosely known as the liberal tradition, which in turn developed from western European and Judeo-Christian history. Notions such as the ultimate perfectability of human beings, the rule of law, social responsibility, veracity, and, in particular, the idea of fairness, are basic to this accretion of moral belief. One finds those ideas in any number of countries, especially those in or touched by the influence of Europe, and in documents supposedly so diverse as the U.S. and Soviet constitutions. Students at the University of Wisconsin once substituted the latter for the former and circulated it as a petition to be signed if agreed with. They were amazed to discover how many people on the street signed in the belief that the material was quite obviously our own basic law. However, I cannot accept that these basic ideas are not applied with equal vigor to the economic sphere. The startling events in Eastern Europe toward the end of 1989 raise questions in my mind that columnists and commentators seem to avoid; does the "freedom" these populations appear to want include the economic freedom to exploit others? Without protection from that kind of oppression, access to the ballot box can become a futile exercise.

This liberal morality is not an exclusive consequence of materialism or of a scientific method of obtaining knowledge, although it is fully compatible with both positions. In fact, it is the product of social experience and, thus, the result of a process as close to scientific experiment as we can get in dealing with the endless variables of human behavior.

The conception of aesthetic value I prefer is also in accord with my basic beliefs, though not necessarily derivative of them. I find most accurate and most useful the explanation of John Dewey, that *a human experience is aesthetic when it is valuable for its own sake rather than for its consequences.*

This concept can be illustrated by a personal anecdote of what occurred while my wife and I were visiting friends. When civilities of arrival and drink orders were over, the husband, Jack, said he had something terrific to show me. I followed him to the garage; he flung open the door and pointed proudly to a black 1937 Buick sedan. It had been restored, painted, and polished so that it was in mint condition. I exclaimed loudly: "Why Jack, it's beautiful, absolutely beautiful! Do you ever drive it?" Jack threw up his hands in horror and shouted, "Oh no, never!"

I realized later, after I had soothed my startled host, that I had asked a naive question and at the same time witnessed a fine illustration of Dewey's proposition; Jack would not even contemplate using this vehicle as transportation. It was of value to him for itself alone, not for what it could do for him. It was, in effect, a work of art. I find it astonishing that this simple principle, which is so highly useful and so elegant at the same time, does not have more adherents among art educators.

Just as this conception of aesthetic experience follows from Dewey's Pragmatist outlook, other basic orientations lead to quite different views of the nature of art and our experience of it. For example, to the Realist, the material universe does exist, and it exists independent of the viewer, while for the Idealist, the world of Ideas is so consuming that the material world is viable merely as an insubstantial reflection of it. However, both orientations require a similar concentration on structure. With the latter the focus is obvious, since ideas are the structure. But even to the Realist, structure is the key element; the world (and hence our experience of it) changes, but its structure remains the same. Structure is fixed for all time, and any vision of that eternal pattern is a revelation of as much of the truth as humans are likely to achieve. These visions are available, albeit fragmentarily, in philosophy, in science, and, most pertinent to our interests here, in the arts. For Aristotle, for example, these activities were means by which we could "contemplate pure form."

These conclusions applied to art and art education lead to elitism and formalism for at least three reasons. One is that the picture of the ultimate structure of the world cannot be obtained by any but the most serious effort. Frivolity or lack of lofty purpose, commercialism, or inadequacies of craftsmanship will obscure the view. Hence, only the most serious arts, the fine arts, are eligible as art; the lesser arts are likely to be seen as inadequate to the task. A second reason is that the vital property of the vision provided by art is structure itself; what that structure portrays is secondary. In art language, the formal qualities of a work of art constitute its essence. The content is subsidiary where it is not irrelevant.

A third reason is that if structure is unchanging, as it would have to be ultimate structure, then it cannot be significantly affected by alterations of context. Neither time, nor place, nor human instrumentality (such as the artist, for example) can have much impact on the nature of that structure. Thus, what we call the history of a work of art, while not unimportant, is a secondary consideration.

The world view of the Materialist also postulates an independent material universe, and this universe too has a structure. But this structure is not only capable of change; change is its inherent, essential quality, and visions of this structure, while unquestionably important, are obviously not definitive. Dewey's general outlook of Pragmatism, in many of the elements relevant to our interest, is significantly parallel to materialism. However, in his view, knowledge rather than metaphysics is the overpowering problem of philosophical concern, and our knowledge of a changing, independent, material universe is the product of our interaction with it. The interaction that is most productive of dependable knowledge is that of science; when the problem is not amenable to scientific procedures, we depend on reason.

Highly different notions about art and its teaching follow from these basic world views. Art is seen as a social construct, serving social purposes, and reflecting the developments of society. It is a part of the workaday world rather than a special way to achieve wisdom. Thus, this world view leads to egalitarianism and contextualism with respect to the visual arts and art education. When, as it is for Dewey, aesthetic response is defined as intrinsic response — valuing an object or event for its own sake rather than for its consequences — any object can elicit the appropriate quality of experience. One might argue that the fine arts do so more consistently since they have been designed specifically for that purpose. But one cannot argue that the fine arts are as a class superior to the so-called vernacular arts or to natural objects in aesthetic potential — at least not within the confines of this viewpoint. Consequently, the content of the art curriculum must be broadened to include a much wider range of materials.

Further, since the structure of the world is not only capable of change, but must change, the context of the work of art (time, place, artist, and so forth) becomes important to the extent that it provides insight into those changes. History becomes a vital property of art works of all sorts, without which understanding them is much more difficult, if not impossible. Moreover, when structure becomes fluid and organic, the content purveyed by that structure becomes valuable in its own right. That Orozco's *Zapatistas* is about struggle against oppression, or Picasso's *Guernica* about the bombing of civilians from aircraft, identifies an element capable in itself of providing significant meanings and provoking aesthetic response. I do not suggest that we cannot value these considerations, whatever our world view, but, rather, that certain views impel us to emphasize particular considerations.

In order to view the ideas I am proposing most clearly, it might be useful to have some sort of template, a pattern of structure to apply to them. To this end, I suggest an analytical device copied in name from the writings of William of Occam, an English churchman of the medieval era. "Occam's Razor" is a logical strategem stating that if we have no more evidence for any one explanation of a problem than for any other, the one that is most economical is likely to be the correct one. I have always been impressed by the wisdom and utility of this principle; consequently I will call my analytical device "Lanier's Scalpel." This instrument is the principle that the essential consideration in any educational policy or practice is its conception of purpose; that all other aspects of the enterprise of schooling, such as curriculum, methodology, or evaluation, are logical and inevitable consequences (even when they are unrecognized as such) of the benefits we wish to see our efforts provide for the learners.

Applying the scalpel to art teaching, if our purpose in the classroom is to promote creativity, for example, we would probably use a studio curriculum with some malleable materials such as paint or clay. It is unlikely that we would attempt to implement that purpose with a series of slide lectures, followed by a pencil and paper examination. One can almost predict on the basis of the purposes professed what kind of program will be presented.

In our own history there have been two major emphases in purpose since our earliest days; personal development *through* art and learning *about* art. This distinction is adequately documented in our literature. At least as early as 1964, in my own book, *Teaching Secondary Art*, the values of school art (which become educational purposes) are divided into: the Intrinsic Value (art is worth studying for its own sake); the Cultural Value (the social and individual origins and function of art are integral to understanding art); and the Developmental Values (art promotes the development of general behavioral dispositions such as creativity, mental health, and so forth).

In 1978 Chapman described this distinction in the following words. Although I disagree with her conclusion, I am indebted to her for the clarity of her statement.

In contemporary educational thought, art is defined both as a body of knowledge and as a developmental activity. Children are introduced to basic concepts in art and to methods of inquiry that permit them to learn about the subject of art. At the same time, art educators are committed to art experiences as a means of nurturing personal maturity. The processes of creating art and of responding to visual forms develop the child's identity and openness to experience. It is worth repeating that personal development *through* art is as important as learning *about* art.[6]

The following four propositions about art and its teaching are consequences of the basic beliefs about the nature of aesthetic experience described above.

Democratizing the Range of Aesthetic Objects

The world of objects and events capable of eliciting aesthetic response is much wider than the fine arts, or even those objects society tells us are deliberately designed to perform that task. If I understand Dewey correctly, he is saying that all objects with which we deal are, potentially, aesthetic objects. Hence, the popular arts, the folk arts, the advertising arts, the industrial arts, the mass media, and even natural objects, are all within the purview of what can and should be studied in the classroom as art.

The most eloquent exposition of this idea I have come across was written by Arnstine.

> Aesthetic quality, then, may characterize virtually any sort of experience at all and is in no reasonable sense limited to confrontations with what are traditionally called works of art. The special significance that works of art do have lies in their capacity to emphasize and heighten the qualities of experience that we meet only accidentally when confronting other things and events in the world. Aesthetic education which ignored works of art would thus lose a valuable resource. But aesthetic education which ignored examining the rest of the world in its artistic dimensions could only result in a sharp distortion of both art and the world.[2]

This does not mean that we must ignore the fine arts in favor of music videos. All citizens and their children, including the poor as well as the comfortable, have the right to be provided in their schooling with access to all the visual arts, especially the fine arts. One might argue that the children of the poor are usually in greater need of an introduction to the fine arts, since there is less likelihood that they will have it at home. Art teachers are obligated to instruct the young so that they can appreciate the fine arts; however, art education should be a matter of providing knowledge, not indoctrinating *good taste*.

My defense of the popular arts and mass media is not the product of personal preference; my own taste is firmly addicted to Mozart, not Madonna. Nevertheless, I am convinced that I do not have the right to assume that my taste is superior to that of any other citizen, old or young. Others have the right to claim that their enjoyment of Sunday afternoon football, for example, has aesthetic impact of a stature no less in quantity or quality than my pleasure in Masterpiece Theatre.

Some small beginnings were made in this direction in the sixties, when, for example, English teachers recognized that street language had currency in the classroom as long as standard English was taught as well. It is foolish to expect some significant portion of our pupils to regard the fine arts or mainstream language with interest if they are confronted with disdain for their own preferences in their lives outside the school. We would be much wiser to start where the pupils are, and they are not, for the most part, "into" Mozart. If no other change were to be made in teaching art but this one, it alone would revolutionize the field.

Eliminating Developmental Purposes

A second consequence of this interpretation of aesthetic experience is that the traditional developmental values that have been assumed to benefit the individual through art activity — almost exclusively art making activity — become extraneous considerations, unworthy of the focus of the art teacher. These benefits include general creativity, general perceptual acuity (also known in the literature as visual literacy), humaneness, right brain growth, and the rest. If we view aesthetic response as Dewey suggests, it is a basic human reaction, pervasive to living, involved in much more than simply the individual/fine arts equation, and, thus, extremely important to know about. Knowledge about such a significant human behavior would sweep all other concerns as purpose in the art class off the board; it would consume all our time and energy.

This change in viewpoint would also insure that art education becomes a vital part of the curriculum of the school. Furthermore, since the visual arts, both fine and vernacular, are one part of what exists in the world to evoke this important response, they must be learned about, preferably in a formal or school context, in order to enrich our interaction with them.

Ideas of mental development through art are also, in my opinion, incorrect. If general mental skills did result from art activity, then it would follow that those who are closest to art, that is, artists, art historians, art critics, and the like, would consistently exhibit a higher level of those skills outside of art than the general population. A moment's reflection will suggest that this is not the case; art people are not usually inferior in these qualities, but neither are they observably superior. Their involvement in art does not give them all those fantastic traits across the board that art educators have been rhapsodizing about for so many years.

Heraclitus, one of the pre-Socratic Greek philosophers, is reputed (by Plato in *Theaetetus*) to have said: "You cannot step twice into the same river; for fresh waters are ever flowing in upon you." This admonition can be applied to these developmental ideas, for while they recognize the influence of individual and group differences among people, they often fail to adequately address objective differences among the circumstances in which the individual is operating. Thus, there is probably no such skill as, for example, general creativity, but rather, creative behavior (if there is such a predisposition at all) in reference to a particular situation. The same individual may be demonstrably creative in one context and totally uncreative in the next. Fresh waters flow in upon you, circumstances always change, and objective circumstances elicit differing capabilities.

Perhaps traditional developmental benefits might be viewed as accidental side effects, welcome if they do occur, but not deserving of instructional attention. I exempt diagnosis and therapy through art, which is now a separate discipline known as Art Therapy.

The last 50 years or so of art education history has been an unfortunate exercise in misdirection caused, in part, by our ideological dependence on ideas borrowed from psychology. Many years ago, a confident but careless pilot took off and flew out in a direction opposite to the one he had planned, giving him the popular name of "Wrong Way Corrigan," an act and name by which he was immortalized — at least for a few years. Like Corrigan, art education has been headed in the wrong direction, oblivious of its principal obligation to the young, which is to develop a citizenry knowledgeable about the nature of their aesthetic responses and about the arts that are available in the world around them for such experience.

Aesthetics as the Curriculum

A third proposition that follows from my beliefs about the nature of the aesthetic is that aesthetics itself is the critical insight, the primary art discipline that should be taught in our classrooms, since it is the one knowledge which applies to every aspect of our lives. It is, in effect, the broadest common denominator of a proper art education. In order to teach it properly, the study of aesthetics should include some art history and art criticism, and especially the sociology of art, as supporting material. I do not see how this kind of knowledge can be provided in an educational context by having children make objects with art materials. Making art teaches us to make art; under school conditions it does not usually teach us to understand art or to know what we need to know about our own aesthetic responses.

This criticism does not apply in the case of older pupils, such as those of college age, who bring maturity and consistency to their production experiences. Here repeated solutions of increasingly complex formal problems and careful discussions of their own creations might provide the information that can be generalized to the larger area of aesthetic experience. However, most school art is clearly another matter. It is also inordinately time consuming, denying the art curriculum of other, more direct appreciational learning activities.

No other of my many lapses from mainstream art education theory has caused me as much trouble as this one. Every speaker knows that terrible moment when one "loses" an audience; I have experienced this moment time and again. This is the sacred cow that must not be questioned, the idea that is unthinkable. Nonetheless, I view this position as absolutely essential if the teaching of art is to go forward instead of treading water as it is now. Let me reassure the reader who is extremely uncomfortable with what appears to be an almost cavalier denial of our most cherished tradition, that I would have a strong component of studio possibilities, taught by highly trained, producing art teachers and generous facilities and materials in every school. There are children on all levels who want to make art and they should be encouraged to do so. But required art as part of general education for every pupil should focus on aesthetics. The parallel might be easier to see in the case of music; general music education should emphasize response to music and knowledge of it, but those who wish to perform or create it should be helped as much as budgets permit.

The majority of our pupils will neither perform nor create music as adults, nor is there any reason why they should do so or wish to do so. There are many other activities just as satisfying, just as fulfilling, just as creative, if you will. But almost every one of us will enjoy music of one sort or another all through our lives, and the more we know about it, the more we will derive from it. I believe the same is true of art. Unless one takes the opposite assumption, namely, that ignorance is happiness or one validates the making of art in the school on the basis of developing mental skills and personality characteristics, a total studio curriculum is wasteful and inappropriate.

If art curricula are to concentrate on aesthetics as content, it is important to clarify what kinds of material fit under its umbrella. Traditional content consisted of theories about the nature of the fine arts and of our responses to them. However, philosophers such as Dewey expanded the scope of these questions to include theories about the nature of all aesthetic experience, or which response to the fine arts is only one particular instance. Consequently, for our purposes, aesthetics is a body of ideas about the nature of aesthetic experience.

Much of the confusion on this subject comes from mistaking the material of art criticism for aesthetics. A simple rule of thumb in distinguishing between the two is that talk about one specific work of art is art criticism, while talk about all works of art, or all paintings, or all architecture, when such talk inquires into the nature of these or how we respond to them, is aesthetics. Particular works of art are used as examples of the ideas discussed; this needs to be done in order to relate theoretical statements to the actualities to which the statements refer. But if the statement is exclusively describing, interpreting, or evaluating one work, then it does not fall into the category of aesthetics.

Anyone wishing a clear illustration of this confusion might compare two statements about works of art in separate issues of the same publication. Both purport to be written from the viewpoint of an aesthetician, but only the first[3] is in that domain; the second[4] is clearly art criticism.

Some in art education appear to be highly uneasy in dealing with the subject of aesthetics, an understandable sentiment. Most in the field have not been exposed to it in their art and art teacher preparation, and most philosophers — the discipline in which aesthetics is studied — seem to delight in making it as esoteric as possible. Nevertheless, simplified and clarified, it is not nearly as impenetrable a topic as it appears at first glance. There is also little doubt that such simplification and clarification is likely to dilute the ideas dealt with and certain to remove much of the rich shades of meaning with which the original writing is often imbued. Indeed, one can only hope that in the process, the ideas engaged are not significantly altered.

Several basic theories about the nature of art and of aesthetic experience have been proposed. Despite my strong preference for Dewey's interpretation, I agree with Morris Weitz that other theories can have something revealing and useful to tell us, even though none qualify as an adequate definition. Textbooks on aesthetics usually cite five main ideas, although their titles may be different from those I will use.

The first theory claims that *Imitation* is the essential characteristic of art. Whether it is simple imitation, art faithfully mirroring life, or the imitation of essences, picturing universal qualities of the object, or imitation of the idea, what makes the work art is its versimilitude. *Emotionalist* theory asserts that art is the expression of the artist's feelings communicated to the viewer; we absorb those feelings from the work of art and experience them ourselves. The third theory, the *Formalist*, tells us that response to art is absolutely unique among human experiences and that it is provoked by the formal qualities of the visual relationships that structure the work. *Intuition* theory proposes that art is the direct, intuitive confrontation of a transcendental or spiritual realm of being, a reality in which reside such universal constructs as moral law.

The fifth and final aesthetic theory, as we have seen, is that an experience is aesthetic when we deem it of worth intrinsically rather than for its consequences. I prefer to call it *Valuation* theory, since it emphasizes the placement of value on objects and events. This idea avoids the main pitfalls of the others. It does not reduce, as emotionalist theory does, all the experience of art to a single one of its characteristics. Unlike formalist thinking, it provides a reasonable continuity between aesthetic experiences and other human experiences. It accounts for the tremendous diversity of stimuli designated as art or as beautiful throughout history, as opposed to imitation theory, objects and events as varied as the sight of a bomb burst (cited as beautiful by Vittorio Mussolini during the Ethiopian War) to Old Masters; from the mass media to antique artifacts; from conceptual art to the paintings of the nineteenth century French Realists.

Like the other ideas above, valuation theory has its limitations. Perhaps chief among these is that the concept does not explain all that we need to know about the process of placing intrinsic value. In contrast to some of the other theories, it is too broad in its view rather than too narrow. As I have presented it, it does not describe the mechanics of the value investment, or what part is played by the intellect and what part by the emotions, nor does it tell us what aspects of the object might promote such investment. Nevertheless, it is a sensible and useful theory; in fact, the only one of these ideas I do not find revealing or helpful is the intuitionist. To a materialist such a position is arrant nonsense, and I have had to be careful as a teacher to voice my disagreement without exposing my hostility, hopefully with adequate success.

The material we have dealt with thus far is philosophical aesthetics, and described unpretentiously it is hardly incomprehensible or obscure. There is also experimental aesthetics, but it would be best to leave that area alone, not because it would not be fruitful to examine, but because it is in its infancy. As an example of this area, in 1964 I proposed an experimental study to the Arts and Humanities Branch of the U.S. Office of Education entitled *Physiological Manifestations of Aesthetic Response*. Organized with the help of a physician and a psychologist, this research proposal attempted to discover those physiological changes which occur when we experience an aesthetic reaction. We hoped to obtain this information by measuring the galvanic skin response, eye movements, and heart rate of several groups as they were subjected to a series of visual stimuli, some of which they had previously identified as aesthetic in nature. I had thought at that time and still believe that our lack of any firm knowledge about so fundamental an issue in art education was unfortunate and might not be impossible to correct. Whether the study would have produced what we wanted or not is still unknown since it was not funded and to the best of my knowledge has not been attempted. However, some years later, a firm in Texas made a steady profit out of predicting the success of popular songs by measuring the autonomic responses of volunteer subjects to a series of musical selections.

There is also a body of thought which might be called sociological aesthetics. I do not mean the kind of textbook sociology and anthropology applied to art teaching theory that some of our scholars suggest. Instead, I have in mind the kind of exploration in the classroom that is urged by E. N. Bracey of New Zealand, who suggests as content questions such as: what makes works of art worth the amounts of money asked and received for them; what people or agencies determine which art is currently significant; what do art critics do and what are they supposed to do; can artists make a living doing art and how did they fare in this context in the past; and so forth. Issues such as these on a very practical level can make up one portion of the sociological content of an aesthetics curriculum.

This kind of investigation, through dialogue, reading, films, and other activities, should also be expanded to explore broader questions in the same area, issues such as the relationship between art and morality, art and science, art and politics, art and economics, and others. Not only are these subjects genuinely and inherently interesting to children, or can be made so by careful planning, but they are integral to an understanding of art, both fine and vernacular, as a social institution.

Finally, there is an area of aesthetics we might call psychological aesthetics. We need to understand what we can about how and why we place aesthetic value on certain experiences. Why does imitation please us in this particular way, or why do formal relationships provoke this response in us? I am reminded of the 1965 Penn State Seminar, during which a panel member in one of the sessions asked the supposedly unanswerable question: what is art? A gravelly voice from the rear of the auditorium answered with: I know what art is! Like everyone else, I swiveled around in my seat and looked at the speaker; it was Harold Rosenberg, at that time the art critic for *New Yorker* magazine. He went on to say that art is what is on exhibit in New York City, London, and Paris. At first I laughed to myself, wondering how such a bright fellow could have come up with such an inept definition. But as I thought about it, I realized it was a fine definition of art, albeit highly limited;

we know something is art when those in the art world — artists, critics, museum directors, gallery owners — tell us it is art. Essentially this is also a perfectly respectable theory of art called Institutionalism proposed by George Dickie.

However, it does beg the question; we need to examine the mechanisms of placing aesthetic value much more closely. To this end, in 1965 I developed the ideas of the diagram below to outline some of those mechanisms.

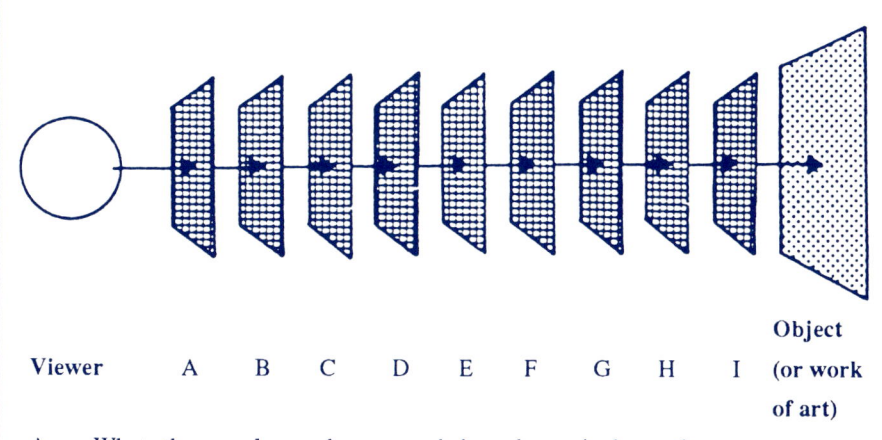

A. What other people say about art and about the particular work
B. The setting of the art work
C. How we have learned to see
D. How much we know about the elements and principles of design
E. What we know about the particular symbols used
F. What the art work reminds us of
G. How much we know about the history of the work
H. How we judge the work
I. What relationship the work has to our life

What we may think of as we look at art.

These are all questions that can be and should be discussed with children. In fact, all of the material in this section, including philosophical and sociological aesthetics, is perfectly appropriate content for art in elementary, junior, and senior high school. What specific content fits which particular level can be determined empirically.

The kind of treatment of art as a school subject that I am proposing is open to the charge of intellectualizing. Where, one might ask, is all the wonderful, unconstrained emotional envelopment in art beloved of art education rhetoric for the last 50 years? Should school art be so cerebral; indeed, can it be thus? I would answer an unqualified yes to the last two questions. Unless we are talking about the amoeba, emotional experiences are mediated through the brain. The more knowledge we accumulate, the better able we become to enjoy a broad range of stimuli aesthetically.

I can see nothing either mysterious or mystical about these processes, although we have only the beginnings of systematic and verifiable information about them. In the sixties, which was, perhaps, the zenith of anti-intellectualism in the United States, there were writers who talked about experience of the arts as if the human organism was nothing more than some sort of palpitating bundle of nerve endings. For example, in 1968, one author writing about film as environment, asserted the following: "... a new mode of attention, multi-sensory, total, and simutaneous, has arrived. When you 'groove' you do not analyze, follow an argument, or separate sensations; rather, you are massaged into a feeling of heightened life and conciousness."[5] I have read somewhat similar descriptions about response to the visual arts in art education journals, often characterized by affirming the superiority of this all-at-once experience to linear thinking.

The author of the quotation cited above quite correctly equated this so-called heightened conciousness with the effects of drugs. It is difficult enough for most of us to figure out, with all the undrugged reason at our command, how the world around us works. Bernadette Devlin, the former Member of Parliament from Northern Ireland, once explained this point most elegantly on a television program. Her interviewer commented that she must realize that the constituency she represented was "after all, not educated." To which she responded in almost these words (and with a musical brogue I cannot reproduce): "It's not that my people are stupid, it's that they are lied to by their leaders." If, in addition, the instrument most useful for understanding how the world works, the linear progression of reason, is enfeebled by replacement with "grooving" or the like, we will have gone far down the road in our transformation into those palpitating bundles of nerve endings. No one would wish to dilute the impact of the arts even if one could, by in some manner removing their emotional effects. What a sound and progressive art education can do is to make certain that these emotions can be enhanced by as wide and as thorough an understanding of art as possible. To that end, we need knowledge.

Using the scalpel proposed earlier, we see that there are those in the field whose primary purpose for school art is some variety of personality change that requires for its achievement a curriculum of unconstrained, unthinking, and therapeutic emotional involvement. In contrast, I cannot view art in the school — particularly required art — on any level as a primarily therapeutic situation.

Contextualism in Aesthetic Response

There is a fourth principle, fundamental enough to be included as a tenet of my beliefs about the teaching of art. Although it does not follow from Dewey's explanation of aesthetic experience, it is the application to the area of art of the general philosophy of pragmatism, a position that has also been called experimentalism, instrumentalism, and contextualism. Kaplan describes the basic idea this way: "... the pragmatic way of thinking means, first, to put every problem into its concrete behavioral and social setting... Accordingly, this is sometimes called the principle of *contextualism*. Every experience occurs in what Dewey calls a biological and cultural matrix, and the conceptions that grow out of and are tested by experience are inevitably conditioned by that matrix."[6] This concept applied to art or to the process of dealing with art means that a work cannot be *adequately* negotiated by a viewer until at least something of its content is known.

Contextualism is important to promote today for two reasons. One is that many of those presently teaching art were educated according to formalist principles, in which what is presented in the work of art itself is adequate data for dealing with it aesthetically; knowing the content is unnecessary or, at least, quite low as a perceptual priority. The second reason is that DBAE, which is being widely promoted with Getty money, is formalist in its approach to art, and the field needs to be reminded of viable alternatives.

I have used what might appear to be a strange word in referring to the viewer-art work relationship; it is certainly not the traditional term used in that context, which is "perception." My strong preference for the term "negotiation" rests on the concern that perception might imply a static, one way process, while negotiation suggests a two way transactional process, in which the viewer is an active participant in supplying input to the event of viewing. As Neisser puts it: "...cognitive structures prepare the viewer to accept certain kinds of information rather than others and thus control the activity of looking. Because we can see only what we know how to look for, it is these schemata (together with the information actually available) that determine what will be perceived ..."[7]

These are the basic tenets about teaching art which follow from the ideas I have borrowed from Dewey. One can, of course, endorse any or all of these beliefs without accepting my initial philosophical premises. However, this pattern of ideas does appear to be consistent and coherent, and it leads to a vision of art education that I believe to be more in keeping with what most of us profess to value as desirable learning. Most of us think of education as a means not only to equip the young to negotiate a complex society, but also as a means to enhance their ability to partake of all the riches of our culture.

Unfortunately, the picture of art education I observe in the last decade of the twentieth century is, to me, most disheartening. All of the major defects in our thinking, which the principles just described repudiate and replace, still obtain. The past 40 years seem to have taught us little but that what we are doing is correct and would be better if only we could do more of the same. There are historical reasons for this lack of progress, and although I am not an historian of art education, some attempt at explanation of our sorry condition and its origins might help to right it.

One View Of Our History

1948, the year I started as an elementary classroom teacher, was a cheerful time. The USA was clearly the strongest and richest nation on earth; we had successfully completed a major war against an unquestionable evil, thus giving us a sense of moral superiority, and most of those who had been in uniform had been released from military bondage. That piece of welcome socialism, the G. I. Bill, gave many of us who were not financially comfortable the means to start or continue an education that would take us further in status and earning capability than we had previously dreamed possible. It was the best of times in many ways.

The teaching of art, while it was by no means a high priority among the concerns of public education, was an accepted member of the curricular family. Best of all, we knew precisely what we were about; our role in the school was to fashion better people: more creative, more perceptive, more humane, better adjusted, and more mentally adept — all of this in their general behavior. Every one of these benefits, our psychologically oriented leaders such as Lowenfeld, D'Amico, Herbert Read, Henry Schaefer-Simmern, and others, told us, would result from having pupils make objects with art materials, if the making was uncontaminated by adult influences. In effect, all good things were already in the child and needed but the warm, nutrient environment of creative experiences to bring them out.

We used clay, tempera paint, wide brushes, and large newsprint paper (abjuring the pencil as one would a virulent poison), collage materials, and the least skill requiring of crafts, such as wood construction. We were, or tried to be, totally accepting of what the pupils made; the art qualities of their productions were not nearly as important as the freedom of expression with which they were fashioned. I embraced these ideas with the ardor and certainty of youth. They had been delivered to me in my art education teacher training courses and through imposing volumes loaded with visuals of the creative expressions of children, many in full color, such as *Creative and Mental Growth* and *Creative Teaching in Art*. If we were fortunate enough to get to professional conferences, we would hear much the same message from speakers such as Viktor Lowenfeld, whose status made questioning unthinkable. It was most comforting to know The Truth; one was released from the obligation to think.

Like some of my contemporaries in the field, I started my education before World War II as a fine arts major, but my time in a uniform convinced me that service to one's fellows was an honorable life's work. Thus, despite my reluctance, since I came from a family of teachers, I chose to become one myself. If that statement sounds incredibly innocent in the cynical present, let me remind the reader that it was an innocent time — a time when we believed that people and society were ultimately perfectible, if only we knew enough to push the right buttons. Herbert Read (not yet knighted) wrote glowingly about ending war through art education, and the big names in the field convinced us that we could literally make better people through the chemistry of artmaking. I knew full well the kinds of horror in human relationships that has been recycled incessantly throughout history; even if I could forget my own heritage as an American of Armenian extraction, I had only to recall the recent Holocaust as evidence. But for the young all manner of quick cure is plausible, and I was young and living in a youthful society. Nothing has been as bitter a disappointment to me and to some of my generation as the recognition that social problems might possibly be insoluble, or, at least, that the solution is not now visible.

On the other hand, four years of military service had another influence on me that was quite different. It seemed to exacerbate a native rebelliousness for which I cannot account; I suppose I was born a rebel on that hilly street in Istanbul. Perhaps because of this characteristic, even in my first year as an elementary classroom teacher I began to suffer doubts and ask questions about what I was doing in teaching art as I did. I was a mediocre teacher in every subject, but believed that art was my worst. I recall vividly one of my sixth grade pupils named Angelo, a cooperative but unimpressive boy of eleven. In those days we relied heavily on I.Q. tests (Stanford Binet, if I remember correctly), and his score was a good bit lower than the so-called norm. While all the others in the class were busily making "designs" (breaking up the paper into irregular areas and filling in each area with a different color crayon), Angelo insisted upon drawing the world around him in as representational a manner as he could manage. These were stick figure line drawings, done with the point of the crayon and in truly fantastic detail. The class stood in awe of Angelo, and I too was much impressed with his drawings and was soon driven, against my training and reading, to give him pencils so that he could make his details more clearly.

One particular drawing that I can still see in my memory is a New York City subway station, an X-ray section drawing, with the street level subway kiosk, escalator, change booth, people, trains, benches, and even the gum machines on the supporting stanchions, all done in a childlike but elegant clarity. It was made with that intense concentration and white-knuckled grip on the crayon or pencil that was the opposite of the kind of relaxed, emotive expression I had been taught to provide for my pupils. I reasoned, or rationalized, that while I would not be making Angelo more creative or better adjusted, I was encouraging the creation of some handsome and fascinating drawings. Was that compensation enough for the burden of my guilt or the disapproval of any of my peers who might find out what I had done? At that point I realized that there was another alternative. Perhaps I should try to rethink my beliefs about art teaching; perhaps Lowenfeld and the others were wrong?

All during the fifties, these reservations about the beliefs of the time continued to germinate, but it was not until 1963 that I produced any writing that came close to my present radical outlook.[8] By that time, others were voicing similar misgivings, people such as Manuel Barkan and Harry Broudy, and I was relieved to learn that I was not the only rebel around. In 1965, the U.S. Office of Education funded the Penn State Seminar. It was a unique gathering of the clans, in which the influence of Barkan and his optimism for the future was unmistakable. It was also the first conference I know of in which the idea of studying art in order to learn about it was introduced to the field since early in the century. This art education movement was called aesthetic education and followed the precepts that Barkan proposed. Most readers will be familiar with the triumverate of art disciplines students were to explore in the art class: studio, art history, art criticism. Not nearly as widely recognized is that Barkan's earliest writings on this subject, in at least one place, recommended a fourth area of study, aesthetics. Since I had proposed that last discipline as key content for art education in 1963, I was delighted to read this and disappointed to see it left out in later literature.

The assembled art educators at the Penn State Seminar generated several dozen research proposals, one of the ostensible purposes of the conference, but few of these were funded. One example of the kind of project that was funded even before the meeting was the 1965-66 Newer Media Project, sponsored by the NAEA, of which I was the director. The project convened several leading lights of the instructional media (audio-visual) field, to present their ideas about the relevance of media to art education, to 50 selected art educators who were picked on the basis of their ability to disseminate the ideas obtained in their own geographical or educational areas. While stirring considerable initial interest, the long term effects of the Newer Media Project were minimal; art educators smiled politely and returned quickly to using clay and paint and charcoal and, of course, occasional slides. One of the media examined, television, on which there was quite a bit of emphasis during the project, was then and has been since then, almost completely ignored, despite the indisputable fact that it has fast become a staple in the diet of the young. When video or the other media are used or discussed, it is primarily as a means to convey information about painting, sculpture, and architecture.

My own thinking as I took over the project was little different; I wanted to find out and tell others in the field what these media could do to bring the art I revered to the classroom, a laudable enterprise in itself. I did not realize until part way through the project that some media had stature in themselves as works of art and ought to be approached in that manner in the classroom. Part of the reason for my lack of insight was, quite naturally, my own training in art and art education; another part might well have been that many of the masterpieces of film and video had not yet or were just being made. I had seen *Battleship Potemkin,* but I had not yet seen *Battle of Algiers.*

Even the temper of the times itself limited my understanding of the aesthetic implications of media. It might puzzle the reader to hear that today's inclusive art scene was so recently quite different; most of us take it for granted that media such as cinema and photography are legitimate art forms with their own viable aesthetic, every bit as venerable as any other fine art. The most hallowed museums exhibit them with no less attention than drawing and painting. Nevertheless, even 40 years ago, this was not the case. My own teacher education program, for example, which required ceramics among its art media, sent me to a department and building completely separate from the art department for that course. Textbooks listed ceramics, jewelry, and fiber arts (then known as weaving) under a different category than the fine arts, often known as the "minor arts," even in the late forties. The term "crafts" was not quite respectable, much less media which were inherently mechanical, such as those using a camera.

It is possible to underestimate the importance of Manuel Barkan in the development of art education after the fifties. Younger than Lowenfeld and D'Amico, he was able to confront new ideas — his own and those of others — in an open and judicious manner and exerted a much needed progressive influence on the field. I am told he was a difficult man to work for, but I have no experience in that regard.

He was unfailingly kind to me in the contacts we had, especially while I was working as one of David Ecker's team in Columbus during the summer of 1965 on the *Improving the Teaching of Art Appreciation* project. I had several opportunities, mostly during social occasions, to discuss some of my ideas on the project with him. One area of concept which was new to me, and it seemed to art education as well, as far as I could determine, involved the recognition of the popular and folk arts as legitimate avenues for art experiences and art content in the school. These ideas were very much in the direction the sixties seemed to be taking, and I had prepared some fiery pages defending my newly found and fairly controversial position. When I put it to Barkan, he liked the notion, but warned me that I must always come back to the fine arts no matter what else I included in the curriculum.

I had written: " ... a large proportion of our pupils undeniably possess an appreciational milieu of their own, to which they respond with fervour, passionate if changeable loyalty, and often more than a little critical judgment. These are the pupils to whom we fruitlessly bring our adult and essentially "middle class" (with all its pejorative connotations) tastes, which we insist upon their accepting ... " It seems to me that the situation today is little different.

In the next paragraph I continued: "Instead of attempting to entice or drag the teenager over to our side of the fence, why not join him on his side? Instead of trying to teach him about what we call the arts, *let us take what he sees as the arts and teach him why and how he enjoys what he already appreciates."*[9] I identified this procedure as "canalization", a term borrowed from communication theory referring to beaming a signal or message compatible with the comprehension level of the audience at which it is aimed.

Later in the chapter I included a clear bridge to the fine arts; the second ten week portion of the model canalized curriculum involved searching the community for places where art objects might be found, including, but not limited to, museums and galleries. Subsequently, I made certain to include all visual experiences that might be viewed aesthetically as proper for classroom art material and connected this idea to the explanation Dewey provided for aesthetic experience. But for Barkan's warning, the ardor for revolt of the times might have led me to the untenable posture of belittling the fine arts in order to make sure that the popular arts, which carried the anti-establishment messages of the era, would be attended to in the school.

There was, however, one position that Barkan helped introduce to our thinking, with which I took issue, namely, that the child making art is behaving like an artist, or the child talking about art like a critic, and so forth. The complexity of visual problems an artist faces while making a work of art and the high level of all sorts of skills developed by years of training with which the artist approaches these problems, make those actions substantially different from those of the child. The same is true of history, criticism, and aesthetics. Thus, we cannot extrapolate from professional behaviors to educational activities; what is appropriate to the schooled practitioner is usually entirely improper for the youthful learner. I do not speak to other disciplines, but in art education I think Bruner was wrong and the application of this idea to our own field can distort both content and method.

However, the store of knowledge and theory accumulated by these various professions is a significantly different matter; condensed, simplified, and linguistically clarified, this material can be taught to every school age level. Learning about what art critics think and do is quite different than behaving like them. This is another example of the unfortunate habit we have in art education of turning to the psychologist for ideas about human behavior in art. In the case of Jerome Bruner, we might better have turned to another of his ideas, namely, that education is, fundamentally, dialogue, teacher and learner talking together. But this notion suggests "brains-on" rather than hands-on and for that reason is often unappealing to the field.

The attention lavished on child art, from the refrigerator at home to LA International Airport, as well as the very name given to it, is encouraged by ideas such as this one. This attention also suggests to the public that what six year olds do and what mature, trained artists do is much the same thing. No one wishes to demean what is often the delightful spontaneity of children's work with art materials; but neither should we leave the unavoidable impression that artists behave the same way. I would recommend a name for the product other than child art, but in truth I cannot think of one.

The aesthetic education movement, of which Barkan was the undisputed leader, had picked up steam by the mid-sixties and received a tremendous push forward by the Penn State Seminar. Those of us who welcomed it were convinced that we would finally (and naively, as it turned out) be able to break the stanglehold of creativity-oriented addiction to studio in the art class. The federal funding of that decade had given us not only invaluable opportunities to confer face to face, exclusive of NAEA meetings, but, more importantly I think, had made us feel that our ideas about education were vital contributions to the growth of the young. But the death of Barkan and two other events dashed our hopes and returned art education to the doldrums of its past ideas. These events were the programs generated by CEMREL and the changes made in the original document of *Guidelines: Curriculum Development for Aesthetic Education*. The former, a regional lab initiated with federal monies, was supposed to prepare curriculum to implement the progressive ideas of aesthetic education. In my opinion, it failed to exploit the possibilities inherent in these newer ideas. *Guidelines,* the original document of which Barkan and Chapman were authors, was, apparently, significantly altered by a team of professional philosophers. Further, the federal funding agency imposed upon the volume the necessity to methodically apply the general principles of aesthetic education to all four of the arts: art, music, dance, and drama, which expanded the volume enormously and made it much more complicated. What might have been a simple readable manifesto of aesthetic education, became, instead, a massive, indigestible volume, laborious even for its advocates to read and intolerable for those who needed to be convinced.

There were many in art education who were unsympathetic to Barkan and to the ideas of the movement. Some held conflicting beliefs; others were restive with what they saw as the ideas of college teacher theoreticians, inadequately attentive to the problems of classroom teaching. I do not recall an organized opposition; such a force was not needed, since aesthetic education died of what today we might call benign neglect.

As the sixties ended, funds for our field dwindled to become virtually nonexistent. What there was late in the decade and later, if I remember correctly, was siphoned off and transferred to the National Endowment for the Arts and used for the Artists-in-Schools program. The cutting edge of new ideas became blunted, and we seemed to be losing ground instead of moving forward. Into this gap came David Rockefeller and his millions, to save art education from its own ineptitude. To illustrate the character of this intrusion by outsiders into a field about which they knew little (except that they could do better than what art educators were doing), we have only to refer to their culminating document, *Coming to Our Senses*. The Rockefeller solution appeared to be that the problems of art education should be left to the wisdom of the studio artist. This was quite a coincidence, what with so much tax money going to the Artists-in-Schools program. It was difficult to escape the conclusion that art teachers should simply step out of the way and let artists take over the show. I found it difficult to believe that the profession at large as well as the national association appeared to pay obsequious tribute to this group, the association with an award to Rockefeller himself.

One of the long list of recommendations at the end of the volume identified above can serve as an illustration of their thinking. This one suggested that we change state laws to certify artists directly without any teacher training preparation. Aside from the very relevant and puzzling question of how to determine within official guidelines who is an artist and who is not, the unmistakable implication of this recommendation (and some of the others) is that art education as a study is quite useless, contains no unique ingredients, and is easily replaced with art making. Telling us we had no distinct integrity as a field should have raised a howl of protest. It did not. For one reason, there were several visible art educators who either agreed with this position or who found it advantageous to work with or for the Rockefeller group. For another, it seemed as if much of the field was literally terrified of the money and power these interlopers represented. It is interesting to note that the reaction of the field to the second and more recent intrusion from the private sector, the Getty Trust program, is substantially different. In any case, art education was so fragmented and diverse in its ideas and in such constant turmoil that the Rockefeller group seemed to sink into the bottomless bog of our confused affairs and disappear. Their activity today is either minimal or non-existent. Perhaps they lost interest; I am not sure.

Parallel to this effort from the private sector, with funding primarily from the taxpayer, was a large and active Artists-in-Schools program, into which several millions of dollars were poured over the years. All this money may have been helpful to the artists involved, but no one can certify the benefits to the children. One evaluative study by a private arts group several years after the program's inception was patently biased; one of its peculiarities, as I recall, was that it found no problems or significant defects in any of the Artists-in-Schools programs it reviewed. In my opinion, the program may well have done more harm than good.

It is likely that artists in the classroom interfered with whatever time the art teacher might devote to learning about response to art; artists, with good reason, concentrate on the making of art. Moreover, education is the kind of enterprise that requires careful planning, a process that would not have been followed consistently. Also, the introduction of an artist into the classroom is insulting to art teachers who are often artists themselves, although my understanding is that teachers, on the whole, were highly cooperative. The occasional rationale that the artist has some arcane, magical quality that the teacher cannot possibly duplicate, is complete nonsense. This notion was actually articulated by Allan Kaprow at the Penn State Seminar, who spoke of the artist as a Pied Piper whose magic the children would follow.

However, by far the most devastating impact on art in the school might have occurred if administrators, having brought the occasional artist into the classrooms, would feel that they had fulfilled their obligation toward the visual arts and would curtail or diminish any additional support past that gesture. For sustained learning, available only through a teacher, this kind of piecemeal substitution could be disastrous; school art is fragile enough without the additional trauma. I do not know if this did happen, and if it did, how often. Finally, if we truly wish to support artists, it would be more honest, more effective, and more respectful of them to fund their making art, instead of teaching it. One of the reasons for the entire operation might well have been that the public funds for Artists-in-Schools derived in whole or in part from educational budgets rather than arts allocations.

Early in the 1980's, the John Paul Getty Trust, custodian of an enormous fund of oil money, became involved in attempting to improve the teaching of the arts and other activities such as conservation and museum collection, by virtue of the terms of Getty's will. The first art educator to act as consultant to the program was Dwaine Greer, who brought to their councils ideas influenced by Barkan and Harry Broudy, namely, that art curriculum ought to be derived from the three art disciplines of studio, history, and criticism. In his first years with the Getty program, Greer added a fourth, aesthetics. The new package was called Discipline-Based Art Education (DBAE), and it purported to alter our theory and practice from personality developments as purpose and art making as dominant method to a serious study of the content of art. When I was invited to participate as a faculty member in the first Getty institute for elementary teachers and principals, I was delighted to take part in this new and seemingly progressive movement.

However, my two presentations at the institute were, apparently, not well received by the Getty administration. I questioned the wisdom of making art as the consuming classroom activity, and I cast aspersions at the previous private endeavor in the field, the Rockefeller program. Perhaps these attitudes were too radical; I had taken seriously a program that later entitled its first major publication *Beyond Creating*. Whatever the reasons for my fall from grace, they soon led to my separation from the Getty consultant hierarchy, which took place, formally, at an expensive and ornate dinner. It reminded me of those old Hollywood films in which the miscreant British officer, who has stolen mess funds or cheated at cards, is stripped of his epaulets on the parade ground in front of the regiment.

It took me some time to distinguish the specifics of my several disagreements with DBAE and their origins; these are part of our literature, unless all books and journals are burned in some future *Fahrenheit 451*. Chief among these disagreements is a conflict in basic philosophical position. My materialism contradicts what I interpret as the Realist understanding of the nature of art and of aesthetic experience that informs DBAE. This latter position leads to elitism and formalism, while my views are egalitarian and contextualist.

One of the activities included in my separation from the Getty program in 1984 was the invitation to prepare and present whatever recommendations I felt to be appropriate for its future. Part of what I wrote in this brief paper was the following:

... I believe that conceptions of purpose logically and operationally control the remainder of the educational process: curriculum, methods, and evaluation. As I understand the policy of the Getty Center, we are striving to develop art teaching which is discipline based, the purpose of which is to promote learning about art, rather than using art as a means for other ends, no matter how virtuous those ends might be ... it is imperative that this focus remain clearly in view ... if we allow that focus to be adulterated by accepting all manner of "alternatives", we will accomplish little more than the dismal Rockefeller and federal government efforts of the last 15 years. Progress is not attained by being all things to all people and leadership is sometimes unpopular.

Not long after these comments were submitted, the Center published the results of a survey of selected school programs, finding, to the amazement of some of us, several that were discipline based. The survey report stated: "The study's findings affirm that discipline-based art education theory has found its way into school practice. The forms of application vary from district to district, as might be expected. But most of the criteria that define this approach to art education are present in all — attention to productive, historical, critical areas of art learning ..." Two paragraphs later the report says: " ... as committed as the seven districts are to discipline-based art education, there is little evidence of adequate instruction in art history and criticism.[10]

It seems to me that the second statement contradicts the first and suggests that adulterated alternatives can be called DBAE and the differences swept under the rug. Many of us can remember how many art teachers delightedly reported that they had been "doing DBAE" unknowingly for years. Often, some discreet questioning revealed that they were, in fact, using a production curriculum designed to promote creativity or some other developmental idea, with a bit of art history and a pinch of art criticism thrown in. Sometimes the so-called art criticism was little more than talk about the pupils' own work. I cannot believe that this was the kind of art education Greer had in mind.

This confusion of purpose and, consequently, of practice, can lead to what DiBlasio very nicely labels "conceptual drift," in which new ideas become blurred and jumbled together with old ones, even when they are clearly contradictory.[11] In the case of DBAE, there is a continuing focus on both learning about art and using art as expression, even though the two purposes require two entirely different types of curriculum for an optimum chance of success. The cause of this confusion might be either a lack of clarity in the thinking of those who speak for these new ideas or their desire to preserve the old ones.

For example, in a definitive paper on DBAE, its goals are listed as: "Development of understanding of art; art essential for well-rounded education; focus upon art as a subject for study." On the next page, under the heading of "Defining

Characteristics of a DBAE Program", is included: "The goal of discipline-based art education is to develop students' abilities to understand and appreciate art. This involves a knowledge of the theories and contexts of art and abilities to respond as well as *to create art*." (italics mine)[12] Greer himself, in his 1984 manifesto of the movement, writes: "When art is taught with this kind of structure, it answers critics who maintain that art education has little to do with art. The artworks of children become examples of concepts learned, in addition to being *expressive efforts*." (italics mine)[13]

Perhaps most revealing of all is the advertising for a new video film released by the Getty Center called *Arts for Life,* which states: "This program ... demonstrate(s) how visual art education can promote critical thinking and creative expression ... in order to maximize intellectual growth and creative development in all children." How familiar this would sound as a piece of 1940's rhetoric and how sad to see it representing a movement that started bravely with supposedly new ideas. It is notable that none of the material cited above talks about production with art materials as a means to learn about art; on the contrary, it is clearly described in unmistakable terms such as: "creation," "expression," "intellectual growth," and "creative development." Once we open the door to the venerable idea of school art as expression or creation, ostensibly leading to benefits outside of art, the ballgame is lost; the same tired curricula of studio production toward the same non art ends becomes acceptable as DBAE. Conceptual drift carries us right back to what we had been doing all along and threatens progress in the direction of learning about art. The followers of the Rockefeller movement must be happy to be vindicated.

Since I am retired from teaching and no longer in consistent contact with others in the field, I might have been a bit more tentative in some of these comments about the Getty program but for an1989 paper by Jean Rush. She made the same point I have made here, namely, that the program is diluting its original structure in favor of political consensus by, as she puts it, reinventing the status quo.[14] That my 1984 warning seems to have been right on target is a tasteless triumph; I would much rather have been wrong instead and be watching art education move toward some of the changes I urged above.

Despite my almost complete disagreement with DBAE and the program of the Getty Center, I must add that some good has come from their appearance on the scene. In our culture, nothing promotes public attention like large displays of money; who would pay any heed to Donald Trump if he were a $25,000 a year short order cook? Also the original identification of art history, art criticism, and aesthetics as legitimate areas of study was a valuable emphasis in a field that had ignored them for so long. However, both these positive elements are being contami-

35

nated by more recent developments reflected in the citations above. I am not at all impressed by most of the literature critical of DBAE, which seems to offer only creativity/studio as an alternative to any new ideas in what can only be described as a giant leap backward. Nor is there really any cause for quarreling, since the Getty Center vision of DBAE appears to be moving in the same direction. The only issue left would seem to be how many creative children can dance on the point of a paintbrush.

Randomly Organized Opinions

The Apotheosis of Art Education

One of our most regrettable occasional tendencies is the deification of both the visual arts and of art education, a practice Jacques Barzun once called "educational inflation." Here is an example from a prominent arts person: "Technology without human understanding is like an answer without a question. *True human understanding is only possible through the arts.* If education is learning to grow, learning to choose, to provide a medium of self-awareness and communication, then the integral role of the arts in the learning process is neither contrived nor tangential." (italics mine)[15]

Here is a second statement of the same sort, this one from a prominent art educator:

> *Art education ... can be regarded* as the most fundamental aspect *of a child's intellectual development, a development concerned with moral as well as academic values ... the sense of proportion, harmony, and rightness that work in art makes possible not only provides the basis of what we know, but also of what we value. The conceptual aspects of art help to form the initial realization, and the expressive aspects cultivate a respect for the quality of action. Neither knowledge nor morality can exist without them. (italics mine)* [16]

One can sympathize with the devotion to art and its teaching exhibited in these intemperate rhapsodies; it is clear that society should have gone a great deal further in recognizing the importance of our field and the role of the visual arts and all the arts in most cultures. Even if such claims were true, however, they are certainly injudicious. It is not likely that we can generate support for our cause from colleagues in other disciplines by telling them how much more important we are in the scholastic hierarchy.

Moreover, these inflated claims are inaccurate. There is no compelling reason or evidence in history that "true human understanding is only possible through the arts" or that "art education (is) ... the most fundamental aspect of a child's intellectual development, a development concerned with moral as well as academic values." Neither making art nor loving art guarantees a brighter or morally better person; instead, history reveals a number of Richard Strausses, Francois Villons, to say nothing of Hermann Goerings. By this point in our growth as a field, we should have rid ourselves of the naive notion that art makes one an all around superior individual. This spurious idea is even demeaning to art, which, it suggests, is not important enough to be the sole significant area of benefit we claim. On the contrary, I believe that knowing about all kinds of art and our responses to them is a vital part of living and, hence, a critical part of schooling. Efland said it well when he wrote that we should study art not for what it does but for what it is.

One of the roots of this misconception is the belief that art activity teaches us to see; in fact, it teaches us to see art, which is a highly specific capability. This distinction reveals the difference between visual literacy and aesthetic literacy. The careless assumption that they are the same is a confusion appearing frequently in our literature.

This misunderstanding can cause an unwitting arrogance. Several years ago, while advising a student who had just returned from two years in the Peace Corps, I was startled to hear her say that the people she lived and worked with were, to use her own term, "visually illiterate." When I asked her how she arrived at this unfortunate conclusion, she explained that they could not distinguish the outline of a leaf held against a hand. She did not seem to realize that they could negotiate their forest environment with ease and safety, while she would almost literally not see the dangers around her. The same erroneous interpretation of perception used to send art education graduate student researchers to urban or rural slums with perceptual tests with which they would test the so-called disadvantaged young and pronounce them defective in perception. But it is middle class art, and the perceptual tests these youngsters do not see as well as they might; the vision based survival rate of the poor in their own environment is just as high as that of most art educators in familiar surroundings. Furthermore, these young people see their own art forms quite adequately. Misled by their own teachers and the unfortunate inadequacy of theory on this question, some in the field do not understand that all perception is not aesthetic perception.

Perhaps the simplest and strongest answer to the apotheosis of art education is to recall the words of Mary Stuart. Writing in 1915, she said:

It is the drawing teacher who can open the child's eyes to the beauties surrounding him; lead him on in the field of culture; strengthen the better side of his character; and in the end produce a better citizen ... it is through drawing as much as any other subject, that we educate the mind to know, open the mind, aid the memory, cultivate the imagination, and train the judgement and reason. Then creative power, culture, control, confidence, decision, direction of best emotions, harmony, observation, imagination, accuracy, judgement, order, dramatic force, spontaneity, and appreciation, are the results of proper art training. [17]

To which one can only comment with the French aphorism: plus ca change, plus c'est le meme chose.

Politics and Art Education

Paul Duncum, an Australian art educator, once referred to me as: "the father of a socially critical art education." [18] He started his phrase with a "perhaps", which I have left out, since with the exception of Edmund Feldman, I know of no one in the field who wrote about this issue as early or as extensively as I did. In fact, only a very few took the troubles of the sixties seriously. Anyone who wishes to go back to that period can look at the 1969 "The Teaching of Art as Social Revolution," which earned me some forseeable name calling, even though part of my title and some of the thrust of the paper itself echoed a retired general of the U.S. Army.

The issues I am talking about can be collectively addressed under the heading of social justice, and in that era the Vietnam War and racial conflict were the pressing questions. In my opinion, art education ignored these issues almost completely, writing and talking as if the world around us did not exist. It is no comfort that the fine arts of museum and gallery were almost as removed from social reality. The very few of our writings that ostensibly dealt with these questions did not actually grapple with them, choosing instead to apply bandaids such as bringing the symphonies to the slums and prettifying the built environment. In an era of body bags and burning buildings, this superficiality should have seemed shocking; apparently it did not.

There is a legitimate theoretical question as to whether or not the arts and their teaching should deal with social justice and political upheaval; despite the magnificent tradition of Goya, Daumier, Barlach, and Rivera, those who write about art might make a case for keeping its skirts clear of the mundane world of social events. The best argument would be that of the formalist, who might insist that art deals with abstract beauty and the response it might evoke as a product of depicting social problems is essentially irrelevant to our aesthetic experience. I see this as an impoverished position. Art and its teaching can and should take part in providing what it can that might help empower its constituents to control and better their lives.

In contrast to the fine arts, the vernacular arts, pop music in particular, have often dealt with social materials and in combination with the pervasive dissemination of the mass media might have had some impact on whatever social progress has been made since the sixties. From my access to the schools and from what was recounted to me, I suspect that a good number of art teachers did deal with social problems, either because they felt it was appropriate to do so or because their students were immersed in such matters and brought them into the classroom.

In some of my own writings of the time, I took the position that the art class should be used as a vehicle to examine and act on, when possible, the pressing problems of the period. The times being what they were, I did not think this to be a radical position at all, merely good sense. But some thought the idea to be extreme. As I recall, none of these critics were in art education; my colleagues were consistently silent. I hope that a few even cheered me on; I do not know. A number of students were stridently supportive. Realizing that my ideas were somewhat beyond the academic mainstream, I was careful to avoid the stigmata of the protester: long hair (which I admit would have been simply amusing in my case), beads, and other anti-establishment accoutrements. I did not even grow a moustache until the late seventies and my first brush with coronary problems. I must tell you that a reputation for radicalism is a two-edged sword. When David Rockefeller was given an award by NAEA, one of our University of Oregon doctoral students insisted that she and I go up to his hotel room at the conference and "straighten him out." It took a bit of fast talking to discourage her; Rockefeller may not know it, but he owes me one.

There is no mystery about how the teaching of art can contribute to raising conciousness about and revealing some of the mechanisms of exploitation, since art itself has been used in this way through much of recent history. This is not to say that visual images by themselves have some magic power for delivering social improvement. Like music and dance, art is far less effective in presenting and developing ideas any more complex than the most simple, than an art form using words, such as literature, theater, or film. In the case of pop music, the illustration I used above, it is the words that convey the ideas. The visual arts, like music and dance, promote attentiveness to these ideas and influence how one might feel about them. A music critic puts it this way and even more strongly than I would: "When people speak of socially irresponsible music, they refer only to lyrics. Music, shorn of words, can offend only on an aesthetic level. Music cannot change society; it is changed by society." [19]

This area of thought, which is in the domain of psychological aesthetics, is more specifically the question of communication through art. It is tainted by the traditional assumption that works of art transmit messages from artist through art work to viewer, in much the same way as words. I see this as a misconception, initially, because visual images are concrete rather than abstract in their presentation of information. For example, if I wish to transmit to you the idea of horse in general, the word "horse" will do that quite nicely. The picture of a horse, drawing, painting, or photograph, on the other hand, is constrained by its nature to present a specific horse, an Arabian or Percheron, of a particular color, gender, and age. What confuses us is the amount of ancillary information we are accustomed to obtain about works of art in words, which we wrongly assume we have received via the image. The catalogue of an exhibit of paintings, like the program notes of pieces of music, tell us in words what to "read" into the art work, but we are often unaware of this operation and impute the knowledge to the art itself. In the last movement of Beethoven's Ninth Symphony, it is the words of Schiller's "Ode to Joy" that convey the benign humanism, not the music. Unquestionably the music is heroic, but a regiment of SS marching by might appear heroic as well, if one did not know the horror of their deeds.

Furthermore, pictorial communication suffers greatly in competition with words with respect to accuracy of transmission. If we wish to be certain that the message sent is received with as little loss of meaning and misinterpretation as possible, our first choice would not be pictures, although they can be useful as adjuncts to words, as in the visuals of a dictionary. Teachers would not want, for example, to conduct their classes in pictures instead of words. Not that verbal communication is itself without problems; often the meanings of words become confused, and languages are different. The only almost unconditional language is mathematics, but it, in turn, has the inherent limitation of range of materials. Nevertheless, despite all of its difficulties, verbal language is still the most dependable vehicle for the exchange of ideas and information.

Much the same lack of precision characterizes the alleged communication of emotions, another vulnerable belief in the lexicon of traditional art theory. That works of visual imagery can arouse emotions is incontestable, but that these emotions are necessarily identical or even similar to those experienced by the artist is highly questionable. This becomes evident when one approaches a Pollock, Rothko, or Kline with a mind as cleansed as possible of prior knowledge about the work, or views an as yet unseen work of the same style. Even unbiased viewing of a strictly representational work without the usual base of knowledge, accumulated primarily in words, can demonstrate the fragility of both emotive and cognitive communication. A more detailed exposition of these ideas can be found in my 1969 paper with the purposely provocative title of "One Word is Worth a Thousand Pictures," and both John Berger and E. H. Gombrich have proposed similar arguments. Again, as is so frequently the case with questions in aesthetics, this issue is an excellent topic to raise in class discussion, particularly if it is part of an examination of the larger question of how we respond to those stimuli we call aesthetic.

In writings about the fine arts one often reads that the artist is, by virtue of being an artist alone, a revolutionary, whose influence is upsetting to mainstream values and, hence, to the establishment. This picture might be true of the artists' personal or group life, but it is not an accurate description of the works artists have created in the last half of this century, at least for the most part. An example of this radicalism sometimes cited is Pop Art, which is supposed to have been representative of how the artist stands on the cutting edge of social change. In my opinion, nothing could be further from reality; the preoccupation of that style was consistently with one of the most trivial aspects of social inequity, advertising. At a time when war, dishonesty in public life, and brutality toward others escalated in our own country as well as the world, most artists seemed oblivious, commenting when they did at all, on the obscenity of commercial publicity. Warhol's soup can is an interesting statement about advertising art and about art itself, but it is a low level comment about the problems of society at best. I am not saying that all artists ought to use their art for social commentary; few wish to restrict what the artist does. On the other hand, it is inappropriate and confusing to make revolutionaries out of artists when most are not, particularly when such a characterization misleads the learner.

What art and its teaching can do, and, in my opinion, should do, is to direct affective attention to those social issues that require it. During some periods such involvement by artists was much more prevalent; the Social Realism of Shahn, Levine, and Hopper was such a point. Furthermore, in any period, there is no way to properly understand a work of art without some adequate sense of its social origins, unless one is a formalist. Art education, taught the way I think it should be taught, must examine how human relationships affect works of art; this element of the curriculum alone, inevitably puts us in the business of social criticism.

Here again is an instance in which the scalpel I had suggested earlier can be used to understand the structure of the ideas being discussed. Little I have argued has currency if the study of art is reduced to a mechanism for making children creative or humane or visually perceptive. Even if these ideas as purpose were to be viable, they do not have much influence on empowering our citizenry to control and better their lives. However, if the primary purpose of art teaching is to have us know about the aesthetic aspect of our lives and the opportunities for such experience around us, then the same bodies of knowledge cannot help but provide part of our grasp of social relationships. An examination on a scholarly level, albeit in the area of language rather than the visual arts, of how we can learn about how society operates can be found in the work of Paolo Freire, the Brazilian educator, particularly in his book, *Pedagogy of the Oppressed*.[20]

Art Teacher Education

Given the principles enumerated early in this paper, one might suspect that my conception of an appropriate art teacher education program would be radically different from what we practice today or, indeed, what I myself taught during my years in teacher preparation. Ideally, schools from K through 12 would be staffed in art with two quite different kinds of teachers: those who teach required general art (primarily non studio) and those who teach elective studio classes. Two considerably different credentials and preparations would be necessary.

The general art teacher would need to have a sound knowledge of aesthetics, art history, art criticism, and the sociology of art. Familiarity with studio production in a wide range of media would be included, but being a producing or exhibiting artist would not be particularly desirable. When a specific item in the general art curriculum could best be taught by having pupils work with art materials, or when dealing with some one who makes art professionally would be valuable, the general art teacher would have the studio art teacher in the school or elsewhere in the district available as a resource person. The converse would also be possible, when pupils in the elective studio art classes might need access to the general art teacher for more intensive examination of the theoretical or historical issues that might result from making art.

The studio art teacher, on the other hand, would have to be tremendously interested in making art and in teaching others to make art. In my own college teaching experience, which is not much different from that of many readers, there are large numbers of dedicated studio majors who obtain undergraduate degrees in fine arts only to learn the sad truth that such accomplishment does not help them to survive in the indifferent society outside of school. Only a very small number of artists prosper without the additional income of another occupation, usually teaching of some kind. Many of these young people develop into excellent art teachers once they become interested in the teaching of art, and the credential for studio art would be a fine location for them. It would also eliminate the alleged need for programs such as Artists-in-Schools; these teachers would, in effect, be just that. They would, of course, be more than just that, since their preparation would have included adequate coursework and student teaching experiences so that they would be familiar with classroom situations and children, elements which the untrained in art education artist from the community often knows little about or misunderstands.

Since I strongly believe that any curriculum should be a direct product of a specific situation, rather than a general fiat from a distant controlling agency, such as a state department of education or the federal government, I have noted here only the minimum basic material that I believe should be covered in each (General Art and Studio Art credentials) of the art teacher education programs. The particular packaging, course content, title, or sequence, should be left to the faculty who will teach it and the pupils for whom it is meant, when that is plausible. The idea of a central agency dictating curriculum, beyond minimum requirements, to a variety of school situations and teaching personnel seems to me to contradict the principles of independent diversity we claim to hold dear. Not only are groups of people different, but faculty have among them different strengths and interests which should be exploited by arranging curricula in those directions, if it can be done without yielding significant content. I am uncomfortable with those efforts of my colleagues to construct curricula with all the i's dotted and the t's crossed, so to speak. Even more potentially objectionable, are those carefully detailed curricula known as "teacher proof". Not only can these be construed as insulting to teachers, but at their worst they deny the teacher any kind of individuality or originality in what and how to teach.

However, I think it is proper to suggest curriculum guidelines, directing attention to fundamental knowledge which should not be neglected. There is also the further issue of *arts* education, which seems to have receded from the position in the field it once held. It had been thrust into the forefront of our dialogue by the consistent support of the federal arts bureaucracy and the Rockefeller programs. This hybrid concept suggested that all the arts should be taught together for maximum efficiency and, perhaps, to save money, as noted in the brief discussion of Barkan's *Guidelines* here. In order to tap both governmental and private sources in the sixties and seventies, it was almost mandatory to write and speak from that position, and many in our business did so.

My proposal for two separate credentials in art might provoke the same kind of thinking; perhaps the general credential could offer classes in aesthetic fundamentals applicable to all the arts? After all, if we take a wide enough stance, we will be dealing with insights and knowledges that do, in fact, pertain to all the arts. I am opposed to this idea and mention it only so that the reader might be alerted to reject it. It seems to me that the person who teaches any one of the arts should be some one who is thoroughly prepared in that art, not necessarily in the making of it, but certainly in the understanding of how that art comes about. I have never met anyone who could do this in proper depth for all the arts we have been talking about.

Moreover, there are critical differences among the arts which a multi-art aesthetics course might, in the need to generalize, neglect, diminish, or treat as accepted instead of controversial. For example, the significant distinction between those art forms apprehended through words (regularly, not occasionally, as music is in opera and song) and those that employ images or sounds or body movements. This difference is so vital, both in itself and as a basis for our understanding of how we respond to the arts, that omitting or diluting a careful examination of the issue would confuse an already muddy area of thinking.

Two art teaching credentials and the rather radical view of a desirable art education ideology presented here are far enough outside the mainstream of current thinking in the field that the reader may be startled. That, of course, is precisely my purpose. Some years ago, a doctoral student wrote the following: "We marvel at Vincent's ability to make outrageous (and at once plausible) assertions about nearly every issue we would prefer to regard as nonproblematic." If you agree that art education has not been and is not now living up to its potential in what it can do for the young, then controversy about our most fundamental beliefs is essential. I would add that the student comment quoted above is just about as fine a professional epitaph as I might wish.

Multicultural Art Education

As an assignment in a graduate seminar, I asked the students to bring to class a work of art on which they were prepared to speak at some length. One of the Nigerian students brought in a wood carving about 14 inches high from his country. When it was his turn to discuss the work he had brought to class, he gave a fairly long, highly cogent description of the piece, much of which explained the cultural and mythological meanings of the carved forms, their placement on the sculpture, and the interpretations of the directions and nature of the incising stokes of the cutting tools.

Our first view of the piece had left us generally pleased with the carving; as art educators we have learned to be respectful of the art of other cultures. However, as he spoke we became amazed at the layers of meaning with which we began to look at it, a conclusion attested to by everyone in the class in dialogue afterward. The more we learned about the work, the more we could "see in it." Without John's careful unfolding of what the various formal and pictorial elements meant in his part of Nigeria, we would have been unable to see them as the artist and the culture he or she represented wanted them to be seen. A pleasant carving became a powerful and exciting work of art, replete with the tensions that grow out of a people's social history.

The issue I raise with respect to multicultural art education has to do with degree of understanding; even an artifact from a totally strange culture or one from an ancient civilization could have cues that would elicit an aesthetic response from the contemporary viewer. For example, the cave paintings at Altamira are good enough as drawings to qualify as art works even without our knowledge of their antiquity. However, it is their age, a contextual factor, that provides much of the excitement with which we view them. There is, of course, no way of knowing how much more reaction we might have if we knew more about the culture of those who produced them. It does seem, from the example of the Nigerian carving, that the more we know about origins and social context, the more possibilities for appreciation open up and, conversely, that the less we know, the less adequate our response, in proportion to what is available, what was intended to be understood and enjoyed by the maker of the piece.

If is difficult enough to appropriately understand the arts of one's own culture, much less to learn enough in a school situation to adequately comprehend the arts of another. A culture, the aggregate of beliefs, ideas, values, and practices of a reasonably discrete group, is an incredibly complex structure, and the only way to achieve full understanding of it is through a substantial immersion in it, ideally from childhood. Usually, the more different the culture from one's own or the more removed from us in time, the greater the difficulty. Hence, my view of what is called multicultural art education — the notion that we can learn about the arts of other cultures in school — is that the idea is much more fragile than is often recognized.

There is one type of multicultural art education that one must unhesitatingly support, the attempt to gain insight into the cultures, and thus the art, of groups within one's own national boundaries. Here the cultures might be closer in time when they are not contemporaneous, and might have enough similarities to what is called the mainstream culture, so that learning enough about it to deal with its art may not be perilous. What all of us want to avoid is that pose of easy familiarity with the art of an indigenous minority some will adopt, often after one art history course on the subject.

Outsiders in Art Education

Since the earliest days of our history, it has been apparent that we have been willing, if not eager, to look to other disciplines for ideas which can be used in our field. Some small measure of this tendency is admirable; there are, after all, conceptions about the learner or the content to be learned in other areas which might be useful to our task. However, we have not been quite as catholic in our borrowing as we might have been, taking much more from psychology than from the other social sciences, although the reason for this preference might have been that the former developed earlier than the others. Also, we have almost completely ignored philosophy, perhaps because it has been made unduly esoteric by its practitioners and because most art educators have been ill prepared by their academic preparation to deal with it.

On the other hand, we have sometimes avidly embraced the other art disciplines: studio, history, and criticism, uncritically accepting their pronouncements about the teaching of art. Occasional instances of this bending of the intellectual knee have been so extreme as to make it appear as if we suffered from a serious case of inferiority. This condition is in direct contradiction to the equally unwelcome arrogance some of our writers manifest, as noted earlier, and the ambivalence cannot possibly help our credibility.

One illustration of this self-imposed inferiority can be found in the way we allow outsiders to use the journals in art education, without insisting that they pay adequate attention to the history of ideas in our field. One has simply to look at the bibliography and the footnotes of a paper to see if there are entries from the literature of art education. At times, the author will argue some point, sometimes valid and significant, but one that has been dealt with by art educators recently enough so that anyone writing about the field should be familiar with it. A good rule of thumb to apply, and one that I have applied as a member of the review board for some of our journals, is to ask ourselves if we would accept such a paper from an undergraduate art education major, or expect the student to have a better knowledge of the field? If those outside of art education wish to share their wisdom about our field with us, they should do us the courtesy of becoming conversant with what we have been saying, even if only to refute it. When the shoe is on the other foot, I suspect that such documentation is commonly required.

This ill advised deference to outsiders is also noticable at our conferences; I have sat repeatedly at our meetings and listened to an artist, an art historian, or a psychologist, who has no sense of what is involved in confronting a roomful of pupils in an art class and who has little awareness of what those who do have said about it, lecture us about solutions to our professional problems. Just check any NAEA conference program. Rudolf Arnheim used to be one of our conference favorites; now it is Howard Gardner. I remember some years ago listening to a potter tell us quite succinctly that all one had to do to become a first rate art teacher was to become a first rate artist. One might think that the huge audience of art teachers would balk at such nonsense. Even if one had no particular pride in one's own profession, survival alone dictated that we deny her words. Instead, the audience clapped madly.

It is disturbing to note that the Getty program is veering in this direction: their recent advertising of publications on art education features people such as Kaagen, Broudy, Gardner, and Arnheim. While they might have ideas of interest and relevance to our field, it is unlikely that they will have more than a small familiarity with our literature, nor will they always be aware that some of these ideas have already been engaged by our own people. There seems to be every reason to recommend that we be more professionally parochial; in fact, this is one of the positions I urged on the Getty leadership in my parting paper.

One can suspect several possible reasons for this *meaculpa* attitude among art educators. We are, after all, a minor, often ignored area in the larger scheme of education. We have also been unable, during the last 30 years or so, to produce a respectable number of "authorities" who speak for the field. Nor does it help that we are endlessly divided; few seem to agree with another, and each of us seems to be off and running on some individual and unique bent, often culled from some other discipline.

Whatever the reasons may be, the condition is not a healthy one. We should be unhesitatingly confident about our profession. There is nothing at all inferior about art in human affairs, and we should be proud of our role as mentors for it among the young, if we rid ourselves of the nonsensical claims of art education as instant panacea for all the ills of humanity.

Newer Media

As noted earlier, the Newer Media Project of 1965 had almost no impact on the teaching of art, either immediate or long term. In the 25 years since then, technology has developed even more than we had imagined it would, but art education is still not involved in its use in the classroom. Art teaching continues to be about drawing, painting, and the manipulation of other similarly malleable materials, and media are used primarily as "audio-visual aids." Individual art teachers have done some fine things with media, particularly motion pictures, but theory in this area is weak and interest minimal. Art teachers appear to be content to leave film/video, which is a large segment of the world of media outside the school, to others like the local English teacher. There is some small interest in computers among art educators, but it seems to remain small.

Some part of this situation might be attributed to the preoccupation of most art education students with studio activities and the kinds of materials preferred in the studio, in their training as art teachers. This emphasis often focuses the young person's vision on traditional media to the exclusion of other possibilities. While this may be appropriate for studio majors, it makes little sense for the art teacher, who should know how to use every means and matter available for instruction. Further, conceptions of the goals to be addressed, such as expression and personality development, also restrict the kinds of media to be used; it is difficult to visualize their attainment with electronic media. It is even plausible that the pervasive use of visual media for entertainment prompts a disregard for them as inferior artistic vehicles.

In contrast, it is obvious and has been for some time that media such as television and motion pictures are both familiar and fascinating to the young, the former from early childhood. This interest could be used as motivation, to provoke a desire to learn about art or to make it, and for instruction as well, both about the media themselves and the visual arts.

Even after the Newer Media Project, when I wrote enthusiastically about the use of film in the classroom (video was merely a puny sibling at that point), I mistakenly placed it squarely among the visual arts, where many art people still locate it. As I thought and read on the subject, I realized that I was entirely incorrect in doing so and that film/video was undeniably a separate art form, with characteristics so different from the visual arts that to include it with them was to misunderstand its nature and to misinform students. I corrected this error in a later publication.

The apparent points of commonality between the two art forms are that they are both visual — indeed, usually pictorial — and that they both employ some of the same compositional dynamics. However, drama, dance, and even literature are also apprehended visually, at least initially, and the first two are even pictorial in some sense, yet no one places them in the category of the visual arts. As to composition, there is so much more to be considered in film/video, that this superficial resemblence is completely overshadowed. These media have one preeminent characteristic which the visual arts do not inherently possess, that of sequence, or changing over time. There have been attempts to bridge this gap, such as the mobile, for example, where the image does change over time and such alteration is an inherent element of its design. Futurism in painting is another example, as is any progression of images as in a comic strip or the Bayeux Tapestry. However, these are only marginally successful at best, and the visual arts remain a spatial rather than a temporal art form, reminding us that Goethe called architecture "frozen music."

Almost as significant a distinction is that film/video potentially combines all the other art forms in its natural exposition; it can use literature, drama, dance, music, and visual art, each as a part of what it presents to the viewer. Further, this facility, together with its sequential character, generates a third capability that the visual arts do not have: it can tell a story or deal with the origins and consequences of an idea over time. Like music, the visual arts are potent arousal mechanisms, but they are weak in narrative and analysis. This does not make art inferior to film/video, merely different, and when that difference is not recognized and explained, pupils might be misled in the area of aesthetics, where clarity and accuracy are critical.

Recent technical developments seem to make the functional superiority of video over film for school use in the art class unquestionable. Film does have a higher quality of visual image, but, apparently, high definition videos will greatly lessen this disparity. Some video cameras allow the final image to be monitored as it is shot, unlike most film cameras limited to a viewfinder. Video is ready to be seen immediately, while film must be developed, and both sound in general and lip-sound synchronization are automatic with the former. Combined with the reusability of videotape and the accessibility of a vast number of motion pictures of all sorts on the inexpensive medium of the video cassette, these advantages tip the scale even further. They make it possible, for example, for the art teacher or the students to tape an exhibit of student art to send to another city or another country with compatible equipment. There is, of course, a considerable loss of those qualitative experiences that make the original image unique; Howard Conant has insisted on this point for many years, and he is quite correct. On the other hand, as long as it is impossible to transport an art class to the Louvre, or bring its art works here, video will have to be tolerated as a substitute, the quality of the present screened image notwithstanding.

Other newer media forms such as varieties of audio-visual hardware and computers seem to me to be of small consequence to art education except in special circumstances. Computer aficionados in the field might be upset by this seemingly casual dismissal of their interest. However, only 20 years ago, programmed instruction appeared to be so pervasive and threatening to education that media savants wrote papers about the inevitability of schools with audio-visual carrels replacing teachers. By now the movement has virtually disappeared; the involvements of the computer in art teaching will do the same.

One significant contribution of the computer, or of computer-like technology, to our field, which I wrote about in 1966, has never been realized and probably will not be for many years. Computer technology could be used to store important visual art images so that they could be recalled instantly by art teachers on a classroom screen. The ubiquitous box of slides would become a list of numbers, and all the art we need or like to refer to would be quickly available. There is no lack of technology for this process; only the will to get it done and the funding are missing. I would myself store all art and art-related images, since the vast number which might seem daunting to some is no threat to the computer.

Finally, in the sense that I will be talking about them in the rest of this section, there is no substantial difference between motion pictures and video. Both are able to depict a series of events or explore the ramifications of an idea. Some portion of our television viewing is made up of watching films on that screen, films made initially for viewing in a theater. If we combine both media under the general title of film, we have an art form with a history of almost a century and a track record of some superb examinations of the human race. Teachers of literature sometimes suggest a sizeable number of books which all pupils ought to read and discuss, not as exemplars of literature as an art form, but as repositories of important ideas about living. I believe that there are motion pictures that perform the same function, should be used in the same way, and, incidentally, are aesthetic experiences in cinematic art as well. They call attention to particular human concerns and arouse our emotions about them. For example, the simple theft of a bicycle, on which the owner depends for his livelihood, in the 1949 Italian film *Bicycle Thief*, becomes, through the medium of dramatic narrative, music, gesture, portrayal by the actors, and cinematography, a momentously sad event. We care about the characters and, hence, empathize with their misfortune and are prepared for dialogue about the moral issue of theft, if that is appropriate.

Teachers of English and of social studies sometimes include film as literature in their curricula for the purpose described above. While I would not suggest that, if it is not done elsewhere in the school, it is the art teacher's job to do it, I would recommend that those teachers who do recognize the opportunity and the responsibility might deal with such films as catalysts for exploring human and social questions. Readers who are interested in this idea will have their own preferences, but might wish to look at another list for comparison. There are some reservations that should be noted. One is that most of the films I will mention are undeniably graphic in their treatment of human sexuality. Another is that a few are politically troublesome. I do not know the answers to the questions these observations raise as to the use of these films in the classroom, except to advise that it is better to err on the side of caution. One cannot help students if one is not there to do it.

While it is clearly not enough to examine the technical aspects of film, from *auteur* theory to lighting, technical dialogue is inherently interesting and can be useful to prepare the viewer for more insightful subsequent viewings. In this the educational use of film is little different from what I recommend for teaching art. However, a high degree of technical knowledge is not necessary; the issue here is to use the content to examine the ways in which we live.

With the reservations noted above, the following seem to me to be among those cinematic documents the art teacher can use for the purpose I recommended. *The Battle of Algiers* has much to say about liberation from oppression and says it with honesty. Directed by Gillo Pontecorvo and crafted with high competence, it should be easily understood by young people. The Turkish filmmaker Yilmaz Guney directed *Yol*, which is about the position of women in a quasi-feudal society. John Ford's *Grapes of Wrath* (from the Steinbeck novel, which should be required reading for all students as well) confronts social morality, and Tony Richardson's *Loneliness of a Long Distance Runner* describes some of the moral power of existentialism. *Blow-Up* asks questions about illusion and reality, and *The Informer* is about 30 pieces of silver. The American *All Quiet on the Western Front*, the Russian *Ballad of a Soldier*, the Australian *Gallipoli*, and the British *Bridge on the River Kwai* say what has to be said about war. *Open City* gives us fascism, and *Bicycle Thief* some of the consequences of inhumanity. A little recognized gem, *Five Easy Pieces* (often remembered for its delightful diner scene), undresses our society, and the even less known *Medium Cool*, does the same thing in a different way. Since we are talking about education, I strongly recommend *Stand and Deliver* as a superb exposition of the passion of teaching.

I have omitted some of the usual classics such as *Potemkin, Birth of a Nationa*, or *Citizen Kane,* but I mean them no disrespect; they are studied as much, if not more, for their filmic craftsmanship than for their message, and the former is not the issue at hand. Nor is this short list of films rank ordered or calculated to represent every major filmmaking country. That their spread is so geographically wide is a tribute to the universal power of the movies. Nor do I intend to demean the value of entertainment, but that too is something different than what I have been talking about. I know of no more absorbing films than the two *Godfather*'s, but they appear to me to have less material that speaks broadly to human problems. Finally, what has been described above can be done with any art form including the visual arts. However, film is an unusually powerful medium for this kind of education. It is also the kind of teaching that requires a high priority in the mind of the art teacher; lip service would be worse than useless.

Repeat Performance

A favorite end-of-career question is: If you had it to do over again, what would you change? I remember a somewhat similar inquiry directed at a doctoral candidate during her final oral. I was not the chair, but since she was an art education student, I was on the committee. One of the members asked her if she could do the study over again, what would she do differently? After a moment's thought the candidate confidently answered: Nothing. To my horror, when we went out of the room into executive session, the committee almost failed her for that answer.

Not wanting to commit her gaffe, I hasten to affirm that there are a few things I would change. One is that I would make sure to take some lessons in diplomacy from an expert. Unintentionally and unaware, I seem to have come across in many situations over the years as a "heavy", in the old cowboy movie sense of the word. Close friends like James D. Smith have tried to tone down my abrasiveness (if that is the right word for it), but although I have learned more from James than from anyone else, he did not succeed in curing me of it. Part of it, I like to think, comes from my passion for intellectual independence; those who prize freedom of thought, sometimes tend to be almost intolerant in its defence. Somewhere along the line, I should have learned how to bend with the wind a bit, rather than to bounce back so vigorously. It is not as if I had no models around me for such political skill; James Smith himself is one. In later years, I could watch the consummate competence of another good friend, Ronald MacGregor. No one tells Ron what to think, yet he does not have my reputation for feistiness. Other models in this context could have been Kenneth Marantz and David Templeton, both friends of long standing. Despite these fine examples, I seem to have trod on more toes than I needed to have done.

Another alternative I might have pursued is the building of a personal power base in the field, an action I have carefully, if not sometimes disdainfully, avoided.

Those who could have been helped by political strength, mainly doctoral graduates, were for the most part left to their own devices when it came to string pulling from me. They knew this would happen, so it was not entirely a disservice; if they chose to work with me, it was a choice based solely on personality and ideology. They were a superb group, and I would not exchange them for any other group, anywhere, anytime, but I might have provided more help to them as others in the profession were doing. Perhaps my fear of contamination by the corruption of our time was exaggerated.

By far the most potent change in behavior I would wish to adopt if I had it to do over again, has to do with the degree of importance I ascribed to my profession. For 40 years I let the pressures of classroom and office (many more in the latter than in the former) get to me, with what were probably unfortunate results affecting my health. It is easy now, of course, to recognize my error and to advise others starting out to approach the job differently; I am not at all sure I could do that myself, even knowing what I do. Clearly, it would have been healthier to adopt some of the humor with which a number of Canadian art educators have sometimes dealt with the field. I refer in particular to the several issues of the British Columbia art teachers journal, which poked fun at both ideas and people. Not only were these wonderfully refreshing, but they served to relax our pretentiousness. I know of no other instance of sustained humor in our writing and salute Canada for it, as I do for much else.

In contradiction to the aggressiveness noted above, there are some instances in which I should have been less concerned with giving offence and should have opened up with the heaviest artillery I could muster. Like every other aspect of human endeavor, art education commits some arrant stupidities, practices so absurd that they should be challenged. One example is the occasional invitation to politicians and bureaucrats to make some sort of statement about art teaching. Some years ago, NAEA had an entire issue of the Journal devoted to such manifestos by politicians, the leading one written by the late Nelson Rockefeller. To say that the writings were inane is to be kind. Politicians and government leaders usually know nothing about education and even less about art education. Not that they write their own material in most instances, but nothing goes out under their names without their careful approval. What the authors of these statements often do is to locate and repeat what appear to be the most widely held and least controversial beliefs. Once they are printed in art education periodicals, the thoughts expressed are given the additional weight of what can be construed as official endorsement. Also, some in our midst are impressed by high office, although how they can be after some of the events of our recent history is puzzling. I used to think that the practice I am denigrating was inept but harmless; now I am convinced that it should be vigorously and publically condemned.

Coda

I have enjoyed my 40 years in art education and do not regret my choice of vocation. While I would not mind having it to do all over again, I am definitely not devastated to have left it. I did not anticipate this attitude, thinking I would miss it more than I do. Part of the reason for this reaction is that the roster of players has changed enough to make me feel that I am at a different ball game; when I read our journals or look at conference programs, most of the names are unfamiliar to me. Somehow, while my back was turned, a whole brand new generation of art educators got into the game, and I do not know them.

Another reason for my lack of disappointment at my distance from the field is also a function of time. Age seems to lessen resilience, not only in sinews, but also in tolerance. I am now less willing to suffer fools or foolishness, and we do appear to have quite a bit of both around us. A third reason may be that I have had no new ideas for some years, and I do not like to repeat myself. The new ideas I have had, many of which are represented in the early pages of this paper, are possible stepping stones toward a new and more democratic art education. They were and still are radical enough so that they have been something less than well received in the field. They are sometimes borrowed, occasionally without the courtesy of citation, but rarely recognized. However, the responsibility of the scholar is to try to generate and present new ideas within a particular area of scholarship. If they are picked up and used, it is all to the good; if they are not, it is not to the discredit of the originator. Ideas are always there to be adopted, at least as long as there are books and periodicals, or their equivalent.

During those 40 years, I have made some very good friends in our business. One of the great advantages of being associated with a large, active doctoral program, as I was at the University of Oregon, is that the students tend to be closer in age to the faculty and, hence, better able to relate to them socially. Some of our closest family friends come from their ranks. Further, friendship aside, I have considerable respect for a number of my colleagues, in particular those who have maintained a high level of independence and scholarly honesty within a professional context of what is sometimes petty conflict. These prefer ideas over politics, and even when I disagree with them about ideology, I can appreciate their professionalism. Exactly the opposite is true in a small number of cases, but it is no great discovery to realize that art educators as a group are no different in their range of attributes than the rest of the human race. I salute the former and regret the latter.

Most of all, of course, I am sorry that art education is so very far behind what I think it should be by this date. But then, in a broad sense, art education like all education, reflects the society in which it operates. In fact, in this era of thievery, corruption in high places (and low), and violence, we are amazingly unsullied by comparison. I wish us well. Perhaps in the next century we will begin to understand our mission and live up to its demands.

References

1. Laura H. Chapman, *Approaches to Art in Education,* New York: Harcourt, Brace, Jovanovitch, 1978, p. 17.
2. Donald Arnstine, "The Aesthetic as a Context for General Education," *Studies in Art Education,* Vol. 8, No. 1, Autumn 1966, p. 16.
3. *Getty Center for Education in the Arts Bulletin,* No. 3, Summer 1989, p. 7.
4. *Getty Center for Education in the Arts Bulletin,* No. 5, Summer 1990, p. 7.
5. Anthony Schillaci, "Film as Environment," *Saturday Review,* December 26, 1968, p. 17.
6. Abraham Kaplan, *The New World of Philosophy,* New York: Random House, 1961, p. 19.
7. Ulric Neisser, *Cognition and Reality,* San Francisco: W. H. Freeman, 1976, p. 22.
8. Vincent Lanier, "Schismogenesis in Contemporary Art Education," *Studies in Art Education,* Vol. 5, No. 1, Fall 1963, pp. 10-19.
9. Vincent Lanier, "Talking About Art: an Experimental Course in High School Art Appreciation," *Studies in Art Education,* Vol. 9, No. 3, Spring 1968, p. 49.
10. Milbrey W. McLaughlin, Margaret A. Thomas, *Art History, Art Criticism, and Art Production,* Volume 2, Getty Center for Education in the Arts, 1984, p. v.
11. Margaret K. DiBlasio, "Reflections on the Theory of Discipline-Based Art Education," *Studies in Art Education,* Vol. 28, No. 4, Summer 1987, p. 225.
12. Gilbert A. Clark, Michael D. Day, W. Dwaine Greer, "Discipline-Based Art Education: Becoming Students of Art," *Journal of Aesthetic Education,* Vol. 21, No. 2, 1987, p. 135.
13. W. Dwaine Greer, "A Discipline-Based View of Art Education," *Studies in Art Education,* Vol. 25, No. 4, Fall 1984, p. 212.
14. Jean C. Rush, "The Politics of Passion: Credibility Crisis for Academics and Practitioners," *Art Education,* Vol. 42, No. 3, May 1989, p. 41.
15. Forbes Rogers, "In Pursuit of Significance," *Art Education,* Vol. 28, No. 5, September 1975, p. 5.
16. "What We Believe and Why," *Report of the NAEA Commission on Art Education,* 1977, p. 42.
17. Mary M. Stuart, "Art as a Developer in the Education of the Young Child," *The Virginia Journal of Education,* Vol. IX, No. 1, September 1915, p. 17, as cited in Ralph Jacobs, "An Historical Study of the Justifications for the Teaching of Art and Its Inclusion as a School Subject in North Carolina, South Carolina, and Virginia, unpublished doctoral dissertation, The Pennsylvania State University, 1969, p. 284.
18. Paul Duncum, "Toward Foundations for a Socially Critical Art Education," *Australian Art Education,* Vol. 12, No. 2, August 1988, p. 7.
19. James Reel, "In Defense of Patriotic Themes," *Arizona Daily Star,* September 17, 1990, p. 5B.
20. Paulo Freire, *Pedagogy of the Oppressed,* New York: Herder and Herder, 1970, pp. 186.